CONTENTS 5A

UNIT ❶	2	I'm in the Sixth Grade
UNIT ❷	10	Where Is the Science Room?
Review 1	18	
UNIT ❸	20	What a Nice Picture!
UNIT ❹	28	When Is Dad's Birthday?
Review 2	36	
UNIT ❺	38	Can You Come to the Sports Day?
UNIT ❻	46	What Did You Do Last Weekend?
Review 3	54	
UNIT ❼	56	She Has Short Curly Hair
UNIT ❽	64	How Will You Go There?
Review 4	72	

Reading Plus	74
Appendix	78
Word List	80
Syllabus	82

Mini Talk Look and Listen. ▶ 🎧03

Hello, I'm Brian.
I want to join the taekwondo club.

Okay.
How do you spell your name?

B-R-I-A-N.

I'm in the sixth grade.
What grade are you in?

I'm in the fourth grade.

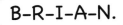

CHECK 04

1 What club does Brian want to join?   a ☐   b ☐
2 What grade is Brian in?   a ☐   b ☐

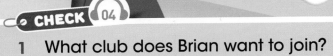
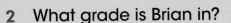

Practice

Ⓐ Listen and write the letter. 🎧 05   **Ⓑ Listen and repeat.** 🎧 06

| What grade are you in? | I'm in the first grade. |

1. first grade ☐
2. second grade ☐
3. third grade ☐
4. fourth grade ☐
5. fifth grade ☐
6. sixth grade ☐

Listen & Talk

Ⓐ Listen and number. 🎧 07

5th grade ☐

3rd grade ☐

1st grade ☐

4th grade ☐

6th grade ☐

2nd grade ☐

YOUR TURN Ⓑ Check, write, and say.

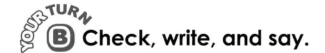

☐ 🧑 Lisa / 6th grade

☐ 🧑 Minho / 4th grade

☐ 🧑 Jack / 5th grade

☐ YOU _____ / _____

● How do you spell your name?

_____

● What grade are you in?

I'm in the _____.

Write & Talk

A Write, listen, and talk. 08

grade   join   same
dancing   fourth

Ann: I like _____.

I want to join the dance club.

Tim: What _____ are you in?

Ann: I'm in the _____ grade.

Tim: Really? We're in the _____ grade.

Let's _____ the club together.

Ann: Okay.

B Listen and check. Then say. 09

Cindy

1
a I want to join the ...
☐ movie club.
☐ magic club.

b I'm in the ...
☐ first grade.
☐ fifth grade.

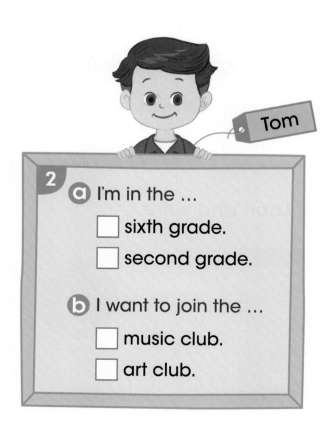

Tom

2
a I'm in the ...
☐ sixth grade.
☐ second grade.

b I want to join the ...
☐ music club.
☐ art club.

Reading

Ⓐ Listen and read. 10

Hello, I'm Joy.

I'm in the fifth grade.

I like doing magic tricks.

I want to join the magic club.

Look! This is my magic trick.

Oops! The rabbit isn't here.

Oh, it's under the table.

1   Joy is in the third grade. （T / F）

2   Joy wants to join the magic club. （T / F）

Ⓑ Look and write.

Name	Kevin
Grade	4th
Hobby	cooking food
Club	cooking club

I'm _____.

I'm in the _____ grade.

I like _____.

I want to join the _____.

6

Build Up

Ⓐ Listen and repeat. 🎧11

first ~ sixth

one – first	two – second
three – third	four – fourth
five – fifth	six – sixth

I'm in the sixth grade.

Kate is in the third grade.

Ⓑ Complete the sentence.

1 Sue is in the _____.

2 Sam is in the _____.

3 Ned is in _____.

4 Hilda _____.

5 Chris _____.

6 Amy _____.

Check-Up

A Listen and check. 12

1

☐ fourth grade
☐ fifth grade

2

☐ second grade
☐ third grade

3
☐ first grade
☐ sixth grade

4
☐ fourth grade
☐ sixth grade

B Listen and match. 13

1 •

• fourth grade

2 •

• third grade

3 •

• second grade

4 •

• sixth grade

C Listen and circle. 14

1 Kate is in the third / fifth grade.

2 Ted wants to join the dance / music club.

D Look and write.

1

A: What grade are you _____?

B: I'm in the _____ grade.

2

A: _____ do you _____ your name?

B: J-A-S-O-N.

3

I like _____ food.

I want to _____ the cooking club.

E Write and say.

1

A: What grade are you in?

B: I'm _____.

2

A: I want to join the dance club.

B: I want _____.

Mini Talk Look and Listen. ▶ 🎧17

Excuse me.
Where is the science room?

It's on the third floor.
Follow me, please.

Are you my new science teacher?

Science Room

Yes, I am.
I'm Mr. Brown.

CHECK 🎧18

1 Where is the science room?   a ☐   b ☐
2 Who is the man?   a ☐   b ☐

Practice

Ⓐ Listen and write the letter. 🎧19   **Ⓑ Listen and repeat.** 🎧20

Where is the science room? ⋯⋯⋯ It's on the first floor.

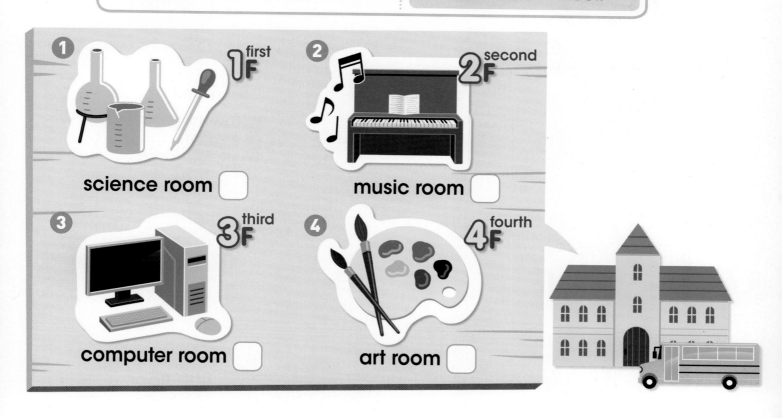

1 **1F** first — science room ☐

2 **2F** second — music room ☐

3 **3F** third — computer room ☐

4 **4F** fourth — art room ☐

5 **7F** seventh — flower shop ☐

6 **8F** eighth — gift shop ☐

7 **9F** ninth — movie theater ☐

8 **10F** tenth — food court ☐

Listen & Talk

A Listen and match. 🎧 21

 **1**

 **2**

 **3**

 **4**

 **5**

third floor

tenth floor

second floor

fifth floor

sixth floor

B Check, write, and say.

☐ music room / 1st floor

☐ science room / 5th floor

☐ restroom / 2nd floor

Where is the _____?

It's on the _____.

Write & Talk

(A) Write, listen, and talk. 🎧22

next to   fifth   on
food court   where

Mom: Excuse me.

_____ is the flower shop?

Woman: It's on the _____ floor.

It's _____ the bookstore.

Tony: Mom, I'm very hungry.

Let's go to the _____ first.

Mom: Okay. The food court is

_____ the second floor.

(B) Listen and check. Then say. 🎧23

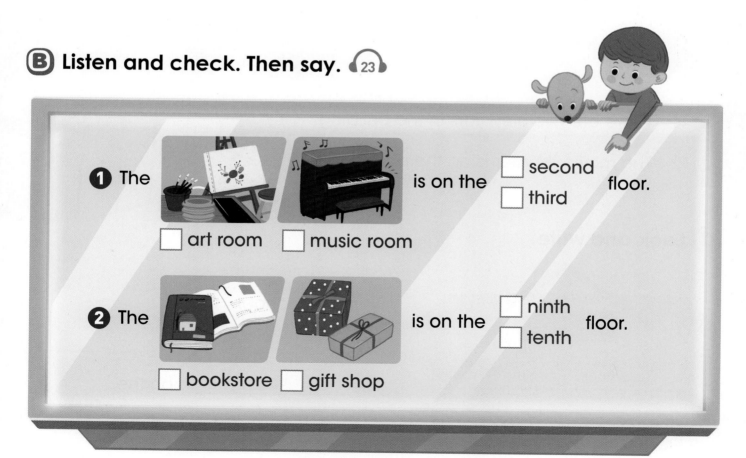

❶ The [art room] [music room] is on the ☐ second ☐ third floor.

❷ The [bookstore] [gift shop] is on the ☐ ninth ☐ tenth floor.

Reading

Look! That's the new building.

It's very tall.

There are two elevators.

There's a bank on the first floor.

The game room is on the ninth floor.

There are many interesting games.

There's a movie theater on the tenth floor.

I want to watch a movie there.

1　There are two elevators in the building.　(T / F)

2　The movie theater is on the ninth floor.　(T / F)

Ⓑ **Look and write.**

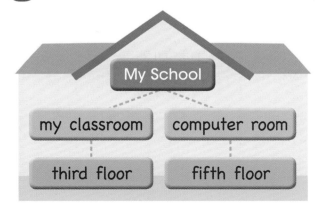

This is my school.

My _____ is on the _____.

The _____ is on the

_____.

14

Build Up

A Listen and repeat. 🎧 25

on the first floor

1st	first	2nd	second	3rd	third	4th	fourth
5th	fifth	6th	sixth	7th	seventh	8th	eighth
9th	ninth	10th	tenth				

B Complete the sentence.

1 science room / 2nd floor

····▸ The ___science room___ is on the ___second___ floor.

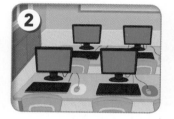

2 computer room / 5th floor

····▸ The _____ is on the _____ floor.

3 music room / 3rd floor

····▸ The _____ is on _____.

4 bookstore / 7th floor

····▸ There is a _____ on _____.

5 supermarket / 1st floor

····▸ There is _____.

(A) Listen and mark ○ or ✗. 🎧26

1 4F
☐

2 9F
☐

3 5F
☐

4 7F
☐

(B) Listen, match, and choose. 🎧27

1 🔊 •   • music room   (a) first floor   (b) fifth floor

2 🔊 •   • science room   (a) third floor   (b) fourth floor

3 🔊 •   • food court   (a) eighth floor   (b) ninth floor

4 🔊 •   • art room   (a) sixth floor   (b) seventh floor

(C) Listen and circle. 🎧28

1 Tom's classroom is on the   second / third   floor.

2 The gift shop is next to the   food court / flower shop .

D Look and write.

1  10F

A: Where is the _____?

B: It's on the _____ floor.

2 8F

A: Excuse me. Where is the _____?

B: It's on the _____ floor.

3  2F

The _____ is on the _____ floor.

E Write and say.

1

4F

A: Where is the art room?

B: _____

2

8F

A: _____

B: It's on the eighth floor.

Review ❶

Ⓐ Read and write.

I want to join the dance club, too.

It's on the second floor.   What grade are you in?

B Look, match, and write.

1
Max / 1st grade

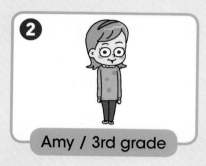
2
Amy / 3rd grade

3
Sam / 5th grade

1 What grade is Max in? •

2 What grade are you in, Sam? •

3 What grade is Amy in? •

• She's _____.

• He's _____.

• I'm _____.

C Look and circle.

1

4F

A: Where is the (science room / art room)?

B: It's on the (fifth / fourth) floor.

2

9F

A: Where is the (movie theater / food court)?

B: It's on the (ninth / tenth) floor.

3

7F

A: Where is the (flower shop / gift shop)?

B: It's on the (third / seventh) floor.

What a Nice Picture!

Mini Talk Look and listen. ▶ 🎧 31

That's a big brush.

I'll paint a big picture. Can you join me?

Sure.

What a nice picture!

What a mess!

CHECK 32

1 What did they do?   a ☐   b ☐
2 What did the boy say?   a ☐   b ☐

Practice

Ⓐ Listen and write the letter. 🎧 33   **Ⓑ** Listen and repeat. 🎧 34

| Look at the house. | What a nice house! |

1 a nice house ☐

2 a cute baby ☐

3 a tall tower ☐

4 an exciting game ☐

5 an old book ☐

6 a beautiful garden ☐

7 a funny movie ☐

8 a big fish ☐

Listen & Talk

A Listen and match. 🎧 35

1 nice ·   · book ·

2 funny ·   · tower ·

3 cute ·   · house ·

4 old ·   · baby ·

5 tall ·   · movie ·

YOUR TURN

B Check, write, and say.

☐ a nice day   ☐ a beautiful flower

☐ a small fish   ☐ a funny book

☐ a great song   ☐ an exciting game

What _____ !

Write & Talk

A Write, listen, and talk. 🎧36

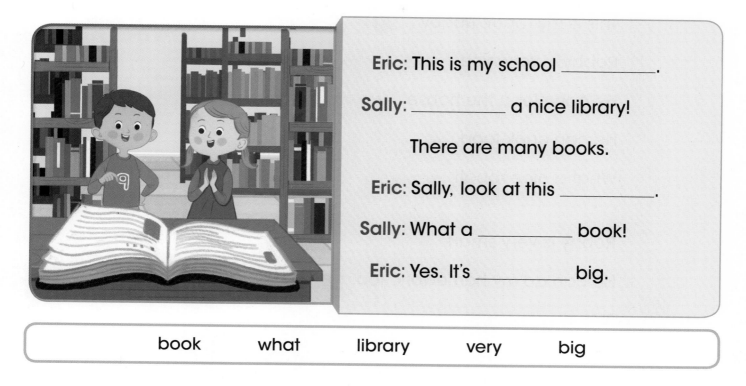

Eric: This is my school _____.

Sally: _____ a nice library!

There are many books.

Eric: Sally, look at this _____.

Sally: What a _____ book!

Eric: Yes. It's _____ big.

| book | what | library | very | big |

B Listen and check. Then say. 🎧37

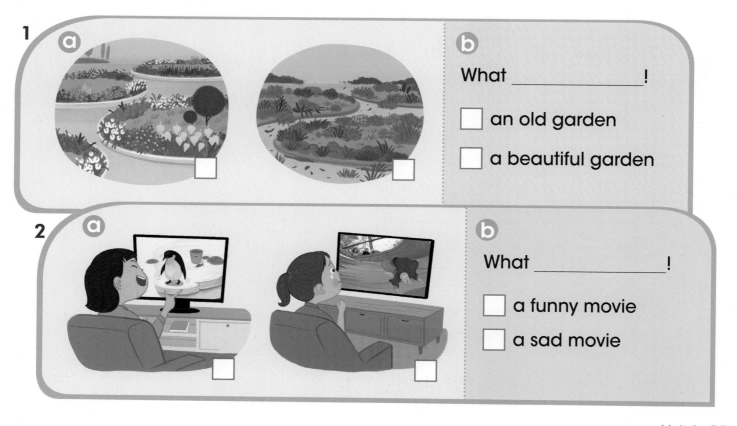

1

a

b

What _____!

☐ an old garden

☐ a beautiful garden

2

a

b

What _____!

☐ a funny movie

☐ a sad movie

Reading

(A) Listen and read. 🎧 38

This is my robot, Robby.

Robby is very nice.

He can clean the house.

He can cook food.

What a nice robot!

Robby is very smart.

He can do my homework, too.

Shh, it's a secret!

What a smart robot!

I love my robot.

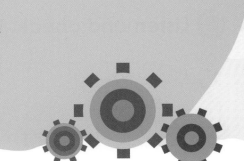

1 The boy has a robot. (T / F)

2 Robby can't cook food. (T / F)

(B) Look and write.

walk
nice
robot dog
play with a ball

This is my _____, Popo.

He can _____ fast.

It can _____, too.

What a _____ robot dog!

Build Up

Ⓐ Listen and repeat. 🎧39

What a big bear!

The bear is very big.
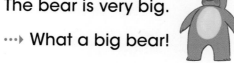

┅➤ What a big bear!

The house is very old.

┅➤ What an old house!

Ⓑ Complete the sentence.

1

The flower is very beautiful.

┅➤ What a _____ _____!

2

The cat is very cute.

┅➤ What a _____ _____!

3

The movie is very exciting.

┅➤ What _____ _____ _____!

4

The picture is very nice.

┅➤ What _____ _____ _____!

5

The tree is very tall.

┅➤ What _____ _____ _____!

Check-Up

Ⓐ Listen and number. 🎧40

 ☐

 ☐

 ☐

 ☐

Ⓑ Listen and choose. 🎧41

1

2

3

4

Ⓒ Listen and choose. 🎧42

1 ⓐ The robot is very nice.

ⓑ The robot is very old.

2 ⓐ There's a big fish.

ⓑ There's a small fish.

D Make the sentence.

1

_____

(what / baby / a / cute / !)

2

_____

(tower / tall / a / what / !)

3

_____

(book / an / what / old / !)

E Write and say.

1

It's very funny.

What _____ !

2

It's very old.

_____

UNIT 4 When Is Dad's Birthday?

Mini Talk Look and listen.

April 4

	1	2	3	4	5	6
7	8	9	10	11	12	13
14	15	16	17	18	19	20
21	22	23	24	25	26	27
28	29	30	Dad's Birthday			

It's on April 25th.

When is Dad's birthday?

Oh, that's today.
Let's make coupons for Dad.

Good idea!

coupon

coupon

CHECK 46

Listen and check.

1 a ☐ b ☐   2 a ☐ b ☐

28

Practice

A Listen and write the letter. 🎧47   **B** Listen and repeat. 🎧48

| When is your birthday? | It's on January 15th. |

1 January ☐

2 February ☐

3 March ☐

4 April ☐

5 May ☐

6 June ☐

7 July ☐

8 August ☐

9 September ☐

10 October ☐

11 November ☐

12 December ☐

Listen & Talk

Ⓐ Listen and mark ○ or ✕. 🎧49

1 May 10th

2 Nov. 6th

3 Apr. 25th

4 Jan. 15th

5 Dec. 25th

6 Jul. 2nd

School Festival

Ⓑ Check, write, and say.

When is _____?

It's on _____.

☐ Halloween Day / October 31st

☐ Christmas Day / December 25th

☐ your birthday / _____

Write & Talk

A Write, listen, and talk. 🎧50

Ken: When is the school _____?

Nina: It's on _____ 6th.

It's next _____.

Ken: Here's the poster.

We can see the _____.

Nina: We can do face painting, too.

Ken: I can't _____!

Tuesday	festival	wait	parade	April

B Listen and follow. Then say. 🎧51

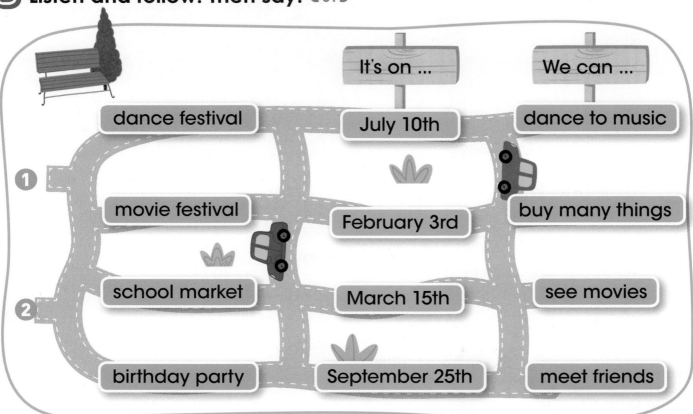

It's on ...

We can ...

1. dance festival — July 10th — dance to music

movie festival — February 3rd — buy many things

school market — March 15th — see movies

2. birthday party — September 25th — meet friends

Reading

A Listen and read. 52

Today is October 31st.

It's Halloween Day!

We wear funny clothes today.

I want to be a monster.

I'll wear a green mask.

Cindy wants to be a butterfly.

"I'll wear a yellow dress."

What a big basket!

Now, we're ready.

"Trick or treat!"

1 Halloween Day is on October 31st. （T / F）

2 Cindy will wear a yellow mask. （T / F）

B Look and write.

December 24th   Christmas Eve

Santa Claus

drone

Today is _____ 24th.

It's _____!

_____ will come today.

I want a _____.

Build Up

Ⓐ Listen and repeat. 🎧53

				1st~31st				
1	one	1st	first	16	sixteen	16th	sixteenth
2	two	2nd	second	17	seventeen	17th	seventeenth
3	three	3rd	third	18	eighteen	18th	eighteenth
4	four	4th	fourth	19	nineteen	19th	nineteenth
5	five	5th	fifth	20	twenty	20th	twentieth
6	six	6th	sixth	21	twenty-one	21st	twenty first
7	seven	7th	seventh	22	twenty-two	22nd	twenty second
8	eight	8th	eighth	23	twenty-three	23rd	twenty third
9	nine	9th	ninth	24	twenty-four	24th	twenty fourth
10	ten	10th	tenth	25	twenty-five	25th	twenty fifth
11	eleven	11th	eleventh	26	twenty-six	26th	twenty sixth
12	twelve	12th	twelfth	27	twenty-seven	27th	twenty seventh
13	thirteen	13th	thirteenth	28	twenty-eight	28th	twenty eighth
14	fourteen	14th	fourteenth	29	twenty-nine	29th	twenty ninth
15	fifteen	15th	fifteenth	30	thirty	30th	thirtieth
				31	thirty-one	31st	thirty first

Ⓑ Complete the sentence.

1 Mom's birthday is on _____ 31st.

2 The robot festival is _____.

3 The piano concert _____.

4 Christmas Day _____.

Check-Up

A Listen and match. 🎧 54

1 🔊 • • school festival • • December 25th

2 🔊 • • Christmas Day • • August 11th

3 🔊 • • Linda's birthday • • January 30th

4 🔊 • • concert • • November 22nd

B Listen and choose. 🎧 55

1  ⓐ ⓑ ⓒ

Apr. 20th

2  ⓐ ⓑ ⓒ

Jul. 13th

3 ⓐ ⓑ ⓒ

Sep. 15th

4  ⓐ ⓑ ⓒ

Oct. 31st

C Listen and choose. 🎧 56

1 When is the school festival?

ⓐ It's on January 10th.　　ⓑ It's on July 10th.　　ⓒ It's on June 10th.

2 When is Nina's birthday?

ⓐ It's October 23rd.　　ⓑ It's November 23rd.　　ⓒ It's December 23rd.

D Look and write.

1

Feb. 6th

A: When is your _____?

B: It's on _____.

2

Aug. 21st

A: The school market is on _____.

B: Oh, that's tomorrow.

3

May 12th

A: The piano concert is on _____.

B: Oh, that's today.

E Write and say.

1

Mar. 8th

A: When is your birthday party?

B: _____

2

Oct. 31st

A: _____
(Halloween Day)

B: It's on October 31st.

Review 2

A Read and write.

It's tomorrow!　　　When is it?　　　What a nice festival!

Look! There's a cartoon festival.

It's on May 3rd.

Date: May 3rd

Let's go to the festival.

Yes. It's very nice. I love cartoons.

B **Look and match.**

1

2

3

What a funny movie!

What a tall tower!

What an old house!

C **Look and write.**

| school festival | birthday party | April |
| piano concert | November | February |

1

Feb. 6th

A: When is the _____?

B: It's on _____.

2

Nov. 23rd

A: _____ is the _____?

B: It's on _____.

3

Apr. 18th

A: _____ is the _____?

B: It's on _____.

Can You Come to the Sports Day?

Mini Talk Look and Listen.

CHECK 60

1 When is the sports day? ⓐ☐ ⓑ☐
2 What will the girl's dad do next Friday? ⓐ☐ ⓑ☐

38

Practice

A Listen and write the letter. 61   **B** Listen and repeat. 62

Can you come to the sports day?

😄 Of course.
😟 Sorry, I can't.

①
sports day ☐

②
piano concert ☐

③
fireworks festival ☐

④
singing contest ☐

⑤
magic show ☐

⑥
art contest ☐

⑦
Christmas party ☐

⑧
basketball game ☐

Listen & Talk

(A) Listen and match. 🎧63

1

2

3

4

5

this Sunday

next Tuesday

December 24th

tomorrow

August 10th

YOUR TURN (B) Check, write, and say.

Can you come to the _____?

It's _____.

☐ school market / next Monday

☐ singing contest / this Saturday

☐ Halloween party / on October 31st

Write & Talk

A Write, listen, and talk. 🎧64

Alex: The fireworks festival is on _____ 8th.

Kate: Oh, it's this _____.

Alex: _____ you come to the festival?

Kate: Sure. I like _____.

Let's _____ at 6 o'clock.

Alex: Okay. See you then.

fireworks	meet	Saturday	May	can

B Listen, check, and circle. Then say. 🎧65

1

The   is on August 7th.

☐   ☐

2

The piano concert is on   .

☐   ☐

Reading

A Listen and read. 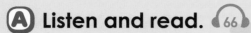 66

Can you come to my birthday party?

The party is on May 15th.

You can eat pizza and chicken.

Let's play fun games together.

Please come to my house at 12.

Can you come to the eating contest?

The contest is on September 2nd.

You can eat many hot dogs.

Please come to Smile Park at 3.

Don't be late.

1 The birthday party is on May 10th. (T / F)

2 You can eat chicken at the contest. (T / F)

B Look and write.

Magic Show **When:**
June 5th, 7 P.M.

Where:
Town Center

Can you come to the _____?

The magic show is on _____.

You can see exciting magic tricks.

Come to _____ at 7.

Build Up

A **Listen and repeat.** 🎧 67

to the festival

Can you come **to the festival**?

Please come **to my house**.

B **Complete the sentence.**

1   my birthday party

⋯▸ Can you come ___to my_____?

2   the library

⋯▸ We go _____ every Saturday.

3   the school festival

⋯▸ Please come _____.

4   go / the museum

⋯▸ I _____ every Sunday.

5   go / the art contest

⋯▸ She will _____ tomorrow.

Check-Up

A Listen, number, and circle. 68

B Listen and match. 69

1

2

3

4

next Sunday	November 14th	this Thursday	August 3rd

C Listen and check. 70

1

Kate's birthday party		
this Saturday ☐	😊	😞
this Sunday ☐	☐	☐

2

magic show		
January 8th ☐	😊	😞
January 18th ☐	☐	☐

D Look and write.

1

When | next Saturday

A: Can you come to the _____?

B: Of course. _____ is it?

A: It's _____ Saturday.

2

When | Oct. 21st

A: _____ come to the concert?

It's on _____.

B: Sorry, I can't. I'm busy.

3

When | Jul. 17th

A: The singing contest is on _____.

Can you _____ the contest?

B: Of course.

E Write and say.

1

A: Can you _____?

B: Of course.

2

A: _____

B: Sorry, I can't.

What Did You Do Last Weekend?

Mini Talk Look and Listen. ▶ 🎧73

Hi, Dave.
What did you do last weekend?

I played soccer with my friends.
What about you, Mina?

I went to the fish festival.

Sounds fun.

CHECK 74

1 What did Dave do last weekend? a ☐ b ☐
2 Where did Mina go last weekend? a ☐ b ☐

Practice

A Listen and write the letter. 🎧 75   **B** Listen and repeat. 🎧 76

What did you do last weekend?	I went to the beach. I played in the sand.

1 beach / played in the sand ☐

2 farm / picked tomatoes ☐

3 museum / saw paintings ☐

4 festival / took many pictures ☐

5 concert / saw my favorite singer ☐

6 shopping mall / bought new clothes ☐

Listen & Talk

A Listen and write the letter. 🎧77

1 ☐   2 ☐   3 ☐   4 ☐   5 ☐   6 ☐

B Check, write, and say.

What did you do during the vacation?

I went to the _____.
I _____.

☐ farm / picked oranges

☐ festival / took many pictures

☐ zoo / saw many animals

48

Write & Talk

A Write, listen, and talk 🎧78

delicious   great   went
vacation   ate

Ted: How was your _____?

Bora: It was _____!

Ted: What did you do?

Bora: I _____ to the food festival.

Ted: Did you eat _____ food?

Bora: Sure. I _____ spaghetti and

tacos.

B Listen and match. Then say. 🎧79

What did you do ...?

I went to the ...

I ...

1 Tina

last weekend

saw many animals

last Sunday

picked apples

2 Fred

during the vacation

took many pictures

Reading

A Listen and read. 🎧 80

Harry: I'm in Paris now.
I came here last Sunday.

Lucy: Oh, really? So cool!
What did you do there?

Harry: I visited the museum yesterday.
I saw famous paintings.

Lucy: Did you see the Eiffel Tower?

Harry: Yes, I did.
I took many pictures.

Lucy: Sounds great.
Have a nice trip.

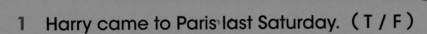

1   Harry came to Paris last Saturday. （T / F）

2   Harry saw paintings at the museum. （T / F）

B Look and write.

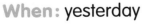

When : yesterday
Place : shopping mall
Activity : bought new clothes
ate a hamburger

I went to the _____ yesterday.

I _____ .

I _____ at the food court.

I had a great time.

Build Up

A Listen and repeat. 81

play - played / go - went			
play – played	listen – listened	go – went	buy – bought
pick – picked	visit – visited	meet – met	make – made

B Complete the sentence.

1

I _____ tomatoes last weekend.
(pick)

2

Mom _____ bread yesterday.
(buy)

3

We _____ pizza last Friday.
(make)

4

She _____ to music last night.
(listen)

5

Alex _____ his friend last week.
(meet)

Check-Up

A **Listen and choose.** 🎧 82

1
ⓐ   ⓑ

2
ⓐ   ⓑ

3
ⓐ   ⓑ

4
ⓐ   ⓑ

B **Listen, circle, and match.** 🎧 83

1
| last weekend |
| last Wednesday |

2
| last week |
| last summer |

3
| last summer |
| last Saturday |

4
| last Friday |
| yesterday |

C **Listen and circle.** 🎧 84

1 Amy went to the food festival / concert .

2 Tim went to the museum / zoo during the vacation.

52

D **Look and write.**

| ate | did | bought |
| went | swam | what |

1

A: _____ did you do last weekend?

B: I went to the food festival.

  I _____ delicious food.

2

A: What _____ you do yesterday?

B: I _____ at the beach.

3

A: What did you do last Saturday?

B: I _____ to the shopping mall.

  I _____ new clothes.

E **Write and say.**

1 What did you do last week?

I went to the farm.

I _____.

2 What did you do yesterday?

_____

I saw many paintings.

Review 3

A Read and write.

It's next Friday.   I went to the concert.
Can you come to my concert?   How was it?

What did you do yesterday?

It was great.

Of course. When is it?

Ⓑ Write the letter. Then check.

1 ☐ **A:** Can you come to the sports day? **B:** ☐ Sure. ☐ Sorry, I can't.

2 ☐ **A:** Can you come to the art contest? **B:** ☐ Sure. ☐ Sorry, I can't.

3 ☐ **A:** Can you come to the magic show? **B:** ☐ Of course. ☐ Sorry, I can't.

played	museum	saw
beach	picked	farm

ⒸLook and write.

What did you do yesterday?

1 I went to the _____. I _____ tomatoes.

2 I went to the _____. I _____ many paintings.

3 I went to the _____. I _____ in the sand.

She Has Short Curly Hair

Mini Talk Look and Listen. ▶ 🎧87

I can't find my sister.

What does she look like?

She has short curly hair.
She's wearing yellow boots.

Is that your sister?

Oh, yes.

ICE CREAM

CHECK 88

1　What does the boy's sister look like?　ⓐ ☐　ⓑ ☐

2　What is she wearing?　ⓐ ☐　ⓑ ☐

Practice

A) Listen and write the letter. (89)   **B) Listen and repeat.** (90)

| What does she look like? | She has **short straight hair**. |

1. short straight hair
2. long straight hair
3. short curly hair
4. long curly hair

| What does she look like? | She has blue eyes and long straight hair. |

blue eyes /
long straight hair

blue eyes /
short straight hair

brown eyes /
short curly hair

green eyes /
long curly hair

Listen & Talk

A Listen and number. 🎧 91

YOUR TURN

B Check, write, and say.

He/She has
_____ .

He's/She's wearing
_____ .

- ☐ brown eyes / a white sweater
- ☐ long straight hair / a red cap
- ☐ short black hair / a yellow T-shirt
- ☐ long brown hair / glasses

Write & Talk

A Write, listen, and talk. 🎧92

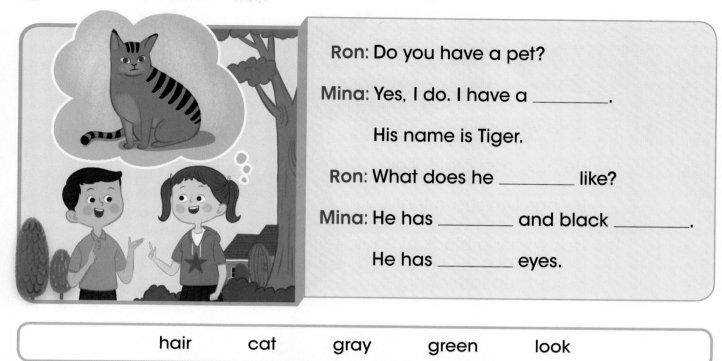

Ron: Do you have a pet?

Mina: Yes, I do. I have a _____.

His name is Tiger.

Ron: What does he _____ like?

Mina: He has _____ and black _____.

He has _____ eyes.

| hair | cat | gray | green | look |

B Listen and check. Then say. 🎧93

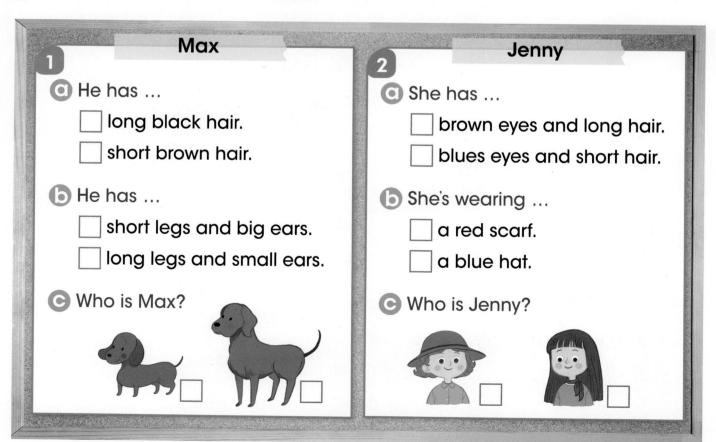

Max

1

ⓐ He has …
- ☐ long black hair.
- ☐ short brown hair.

ⓑ He has …
- ☐ short legs and big ears.
- ☐ long legs and small ears.

ⓒ Who is Max?

Jenny

2

ⓐ She has …
- ☐ brown eyes and long hair.
- ☐ blues eyes and short hair.

ⓑ She's wearing …
- ☐ a red scarf.
- ☐ a blue hat.

ⓒ Who is Jenny?

Reading

A Listen and read. 94

He is very tall.

He has short black hair.

He has two sharp teeth.

He's wearing black clothes.

He gets up late at night.

He doesn't like the sun.

He is 300 years old.

Who is he?

He is Dracula!

1 He has long curly hair. （ T / F ）

2 He's wearing black clothes. （ T / F ）

B Write and check.

long hair
big brown eyes
a blue dress

Can you find Tina?

She has _____.

She has _____.

She's wearing _____.

60

Build Up

A Listen and repeat. 🎧 95

long brown hair

| I/They | have | long | brown black | hair. |
| He/She/It | has | short | straight curly | |

B Complete the sentence.

1

I have _____.
(hair / long / curly)

2

They have _____.
(brown / short / hair)

3

She has _____.
(straight / long / hair)

4

The cat has _____.
(hair / brown / long)

5

Tina has _____.
(big / eyes / blue)

Check-Up

A Listen and choose. 🎧 96

1 ⓐ ⓑ

2 ⓐ ⓑ

3 ⓐ ⓑ

4 ⓐ ⓑ

B Listen and mark ○ or ✕. 🎧 97

1 ☐

2 ☐

3 ☐

4 ☐

C Listen and circle. 🎧 98

1 Sally has long curly / short curly hair.

2 Jane's brother is wearing a blue jacket / a red T-shirt .

D Look and write.

short straight hair   glasses
blue eyes   long brown hair

1

A: What does she look like?

B: She has _____.

2

A: What does he look like?

B: He has _____ and curly hair.

3

Ben has _____.

He's wearing _____.

E Write and say.

1

A: What does he look like?

B: _____ and _____.
    (brown / short black)

2

A: What does she look like?

B: _____
    (long straight)

UNIT 8 How Will You Go There?

Mini Talk Look and Listen. ▶ 🎧101

Mom, I'll go to the beach today.

How will you go there?

I'll go there by bus.

Don't sleep on the bus, Tom.

Beach

CHECK 🎧102

1 Where will Tom go today? a ☐ b ☐
2 How will he go there? a ☐ b ☐

Practice

A Listen and write the letter. 103

A: I'll go to the library.
B: How will you go there?
A: I'll go there by bus.

B Listen and repeat. 104

1. the library / by bus

2. the museum / by car

3. the zoo / by subway

4. the farm / by train

5. the market / by bike

6. the park / on foot

PARK

7. Japan / by ship

New York

8. New York / by plane

Listen & Talk

A Listen and mark ○ or ✗. 🎧105

YOUR TURN

B Check, write, and say.

☐ the airport / by bus

☐ the park / on foot

☐ the mountain / by bike

☐ England / by plane

I'll go to _____.

I'll go there _____.

Write & Talk

A Write, listen, and talk. 106

how busy join
toy shop by bus

Lisa: What will you do tomorrow?

Roy: I'll go to the _____.

Lisa: _____ will you go there?

Roy: I'll go there _____.

Can you _____ me?

Lisa: Sorry, I can't. I'm _____

tomorrow.

B Listen and check. Then say. 107

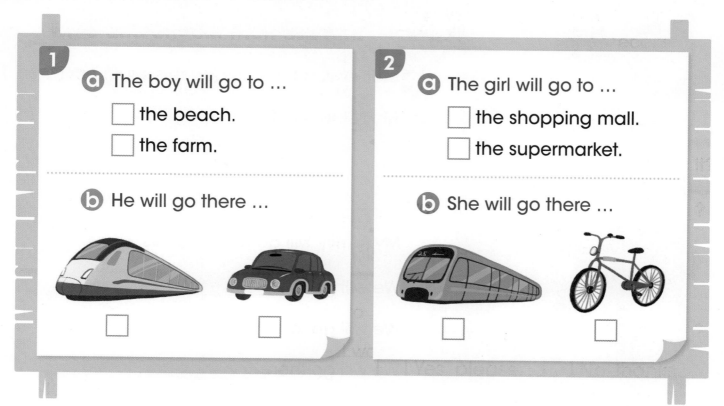

1

ⓐ The boy will go to …
- [ ] the beach.
- [ ] the farm.

ⓑ He will go there …

2

ⓐ The girl will go to …
- [ ] the shopping mall.
- [ ] the supermarket.

ⓑ She will go there …

Reading

Hello, I'm Molly.

I'll go to Canada this summer.

How will I go there?

By plane? No. By train? No.

I'll go there by bike!

I'm in the bike riding club.

We went to L.A. by bike last year.

It was exciting.

We love to travel by bike.

Do you want to join our club?

1   Molly will go to Canada this summer.   (T / F)

2   Molly loves to travel by train.   (T / F)

B Look and write.

My family will go to Rome this winter.

We will go there _____.

We will go to _____, too.

We will go there _____.

Build Up

A Listen and repeat. 109

by bus

I go to school by bus.

I go to school by subway.

B Make the sentence.

1 (bike / go to school / I / by / .)

...▸ _____

2 (by / Lisa / train / went to Rome / .)

...▸ _____

3 (go to Australia / ship / by / they / .)

...▸ _____

4 (will / plane / Mary / by / go to the U.S. / .)

...▸ _____

5 (subway / by / go to the hospital / I'll / .)

...▸ _____

Check-Up

A Listen and choose. 🎧110

1

a · b

2

a · b

3

a · b

4

a · b

B Listen and match. 🎧111

1 🔊 ·

· 🖼️ ·

· by plane

2 🔊 ·

· 🖼️ ·

· on foot

3 🔊 ·

· 🖼️ ·

· by train

4 🔊 ·

· 🖼️ ·

· by subway

C Listen and circle. 🎧112

1 The boy will go to the museum [by bus / by bike] .

2 They will go to the beach [by car / on foot] .

D Match and write.

1

A: I'll go to the hospital.

B: How _____ go there?

A: I'll go there _____.

2

A: I'll go to the mountain.

B: How will you _____?

A: I'll go there _____.

3

A: I'll go to the park.

B: How _____?

A: I'll go there _____.

E Write and say.

1

A: How will you go to the airport?

B: I'll _____.

2

A: How will you go to the shopping mall?

B: _____

Review 4

A Read and write.

I'll go there by train.   I'll visit Mr. Baker's house.
He has short brown hair.

What will you do this weekend, Jake?

That's great! How will you go there?

Oh! It's Jake.

I can't see him. What does he look like?

B Read and write the letter.

1   My sister has blue eyes and long curly hair.   ☐

2   My brother has black eyes and short hair.   ☐

3   My mom has short curly hair. She's wearing a pink dress.   ☐

4   Jane has long straight hair. She's wearing a blue T-shirt.   ☐

C Look and write.

1    I'll go there _____.

2    I'll go there _____.

3    I'll go there _____.

4    I'll go there _____.

How will you go to the library?

bus
bike
subway
foot

Shopping with My Family

Let's go shopping!

What a nice shopping mall!
Dad wants some chocolate cake.
The bakery is on the third floor.
Mom wants some flowers.
The flower shop is on the fifth floor.

My sister wants a teddy bear.
I want to buy a new board game.
Where is the toy shop?
Oh, it's on the fourth flur.
I want to go to the toy shop first!

1 This story is about _____.

  ⓐ going shopping   ⓑ planting flowers

  ⓒ baking bread   ⓓ playing games

Comprehension

2 The boy's family are at the _____.

  ⓐ museum   ⓑ shopping mall   ⓒ food court

3 The boy's mom wants _____.

  ⓐ some cake   ⓑ a teddy bear   ⓒ some flowers

4 The toy shop is on the _____.

  ⓐ 2nd floor   ⓑ 4th floor   ⓒ 5th floor

Writing Practice

> Where is the bakery? ⋯▸ It's on the third floor.

1 Where is the flower shop?

  ⋯▸ It's on _____. (fifth floor)

2 Where is the toy shop?

  ⋯▸ _____ (fourth floor)

Ant's Birthday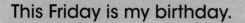

This Friday is my birthday.

I'll have a birthday party.

I picked tomatoes and apples today.

I'll make a cake, too.

Can you come to my house?

Of course!

I can play the violin for you.

What does your house look like?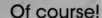

It has a yellow door and a big window.

There are red flowers in the garden.

See you on Friday!

76

1 This story is about _____.

    ⓐ a birthday cake   ⓑ the grasshopper's violin

    ⓒ tomatoes and apples   ⓓ the ant's birthday party

Comprehension

2 When is the ant's birthday?

    ⓐ next Friday   ⓑ this Friday   ⓒ today

3 The ant _____.

    ⓐ played the violin   ⓑ made some cookies   ⓒ picked tomatoes

4 The ant's house has _____.

    ⓐ yellow flowers   ⓑ a small window   ⓒ a yellow door

Writing Practice ▸

What does your house look like? ⋯▸ It has a yellow door.

1 What does an elephant look like?

    ⋯▸ It _____. (a long nose and big ears)

2 What does your brother look like?

    ⋯▸ _____ (blue eyes and short hair)

Appendix

• Regular Verbs

Base Form	Simple Past		Base Form	Simple Past	
bake	baked		listen	listened	
borrow	borrowed		open	opened	
brush	brushed		pick	picked	
clean	cleaned		plant	planted	
climb	climbed		play	played	
close	closed		push	pushed	
cook	cooked		stay	stayed	
cry	cried		study	studied	
dance	danced		talk	talked	
enter	entered		travel	traveled	
exercise	exercised		use	used	
help	helped		visit	visited	
invent	invented		walk	walked	
join	joined		wash	washed	
jump	jumped		watch	watched	

Irregular Verbs

Base Form	Simple Past		Base Form	Simple Past	
be (am/is/are)	was/were		make	made	
break	broke		meet	met	
bring	brought		put	put	
build	built		read	read	
buy	bought		ride	rode	
catch	caught		run	ran	
come	came		see	saw	
do	did		sing	sang	
draw	drew		sit	sat	
drink	drank		sleep	slept	
eat	ate		stand	stood	
fly	flew		swim	swam	
get	got		take	took	
go	went		win	won	
have	had		write	wrote	

Word List 5A

Unit 1   I'm in the Sixth Grade

first   _____

second   _____

third   _____

fourth   _____

fifth   _____

sixth   _____

club   _____

grade   _____

join   _____

magic trick   _____

same   _____

spell   _____

together   _____

Unit 2   Where Is the Science Room?

art room   _____

bank   _____

bookstore   _____

building   _____

computer room   _____

floor   _____

flower shop   _____

food court   _____

gift shop   _____

movie theater   _____

music room   _____

restroom   _____

science room   _____

Unit 3   What a Nice Picture!

beautiful garden   _____

big brush   _____

big fish   _____

cute baby   _____

exciting game   _____

funny movie   _____

nice house   _____

nice picture   _____

old book   _____

sad movie   _____

smart robot   _____

tall tower   _____

tall tree   _____

Unit 4   When Is Dad's Birthday?

January   _____

February   _____

March   _____

April   _____

May   _____

June   _____

July   _____

August   _____

September   _____

October   _____

November   _____

December   _____

when   _____

Unit 5 — Can You Come to the Sports Day?

art contest   _____

basketball game   _____

Christmas party   _____

enjoy   _____

fireworks festival   _____

Halloween party   _____

magic show   _____

meet   _____

piano concert   _____

singing contest   _____

sports day   _____

Unit 6 — What Did You Do Last Weekend?

beach   _____

bought new clothes   _____

concert   _____

during the vacation   _____

last weekend   _____

museum   _____

picked tomatoes   _____

played in the sand   _____

saw many animals   _____

saw my favorite singer   _____

saw paintings   _____

shopping mall   _____

took many pictures   _____

Unit 7 — She Has Short Curly Hair

black clothes   _____

blue eyes   _____

brown eyes   _____

find   _____

green eyes   _____

long curly hair   _____

long straight hair   _____

look like   _____

short curly hair   _____

short straight hair   _____

wear   _____

Unit 8 — How Will You Go There?

airport   _____

by bike   _____

by bus   _____

by car   _____

by plane   _____

by ship   _____

by subway   _____

by train   _____

market   _____

mountain   _____

museum   _____

on foot   _____

park   _____

Unit 1 I'm in the Sixth Grade

Structures	Vocabulary		Grammar
• What grade are you in?	first	sixth	first ~ sixth
I'm in the first grade.	second	grade	
• I want to join the taekwondo club.	third	spell	
• How do you spell your name?	fourth	join	
B-R-I-A-N	fifth	club	**Reading**

Unit 2 Where Is the Science Room?

Structures	Vocabulary		Grammar
• Where is the science room?	science room	gift shop	on the first floor
It's on the first floor.	music room	movie theater	
• Excuse me.	computer room	food court	
• Follow me, please.	art room	bookstore	
• It's next to the bookstore.	flower shop	restroom	**Reading**

Review 1

Unit 3 What a Nice Picture!

Structures	Vocabulary		Grammar
• Look at the house.	nice picture	old book	What a big bear!
What a nice house!	nice house	beautiful garden	
• Yes. It's a funny movie.	cute baby	funny movie	
• There's a book.	tall tower	big fish	
• It's very tall.	exciting game		**Reading**

Unit 4 When Is Dad's Birthday?

Structures	Vocabulary		Grammar
• When is your birthday?	January	July	1st ~ 31st
It's on January 15th.	February	August	
• Oh, that's today.	March	September	
• It's next Tuesday.	April	October	
• We can see the parade.	May	November	
• I can't wait!	June	December	**Reading**

Review 2

Unit 5 Can You Come to the Sports Day?

Structures	Vocabulary		Grammar
• Can you come to the sports day? Of course. / Sorry, I can't. • When is it? • Okay. See you then.	sports day piano concert fireworks festival singing contest	magic show art contest Christmas party basketball game	to the festival **Reading**

Unit 6 What Did You Do Last Weekend?

Structures	Vocabulary		Grammar

• What did you do last weekend?
  I went to the beach. I played in the sand.
• Did you take many pictures?
  Yes, I did.
• Sounds fun.
	beach
	farm
	museum
	festival
	concert
	shopping mall
		played in the sand
		picked tomatoes
		saw paintings
		took many pictures
		saw my favorite singer
		bought new clothes
			play-played
			go-went
			
			Reading

Review 3

Unit 7 She Has Short Curly Hair

Structures	Vocabulary		Grammar

• What does she look like?
  She has short straight hair.
• What does she look like?
  She has blue eyes and long straight hair.
• He's wearing a blue sweater.
	short straight hair
	long straight hair
	short curly hair
	long curly hair
		blue eyes
		brown eyes
		green eyes
			long brown hair
			
			Reading

Unit 8 How Will You Go There?

Structures	Vocabulary				Grammar

• I'll go to the library.
  How will you go there?
  I'll go there by bus.
	library
	museum
	zoo
	farm
		market
		park
		Japan
		New York
			by bus
			by car
			by subway
			by train
				by bike
				on foot
				by ship
				by plane
					by bus
					
					Reading

Review 4

Midterm TEST 5A

Institute _____

Name _____

Score _____ /100

[1-2] Listen and choose.
다음을 듣고, 알맞은 그림을 고르세요.

1 ⓐ  ⓑ

   ⓒ  ⓓ

2 ⓐ  ⓑ

   ⓒ  ⓓ

[3-5] Listen and choose.
다음을 듣고, 질문에 알맞은 응답을 고르세요.

3 ⓐ What a nice picture!
   ⓑ It's on June 13th.
   ⓒ This movie is very funny.
   ⓓ It's on the fifth floor.

4 ⓐ I'm in the magic club.
   ⓑ What an old book!
   ⓒ It's on May 10th.
   ⓓ I'm in the second grade.

5 ⓐ I'm in the fourth grade.
   ⓑ It's on the ninth floor.
   ⓒ I like drawing pictures.
   ⓓ It's on April 20th.

[6-8] Listen and match.
대화를 듣고, 알맞은 그림에 연결하세요.

6 •   ⓐ

7 •   ⓑ

8 •   ⓒ

[9-10] Listen and mark O or X.
대화를 듣고, ○ 또는 X를 표시하세요.

9  ☐

10  ☐

[11-12] Read and choose.
빈칸에 알맞은 것을 고르세요.

11 The gift shop is _____ the eighth floor.

ⓐ in   ⓑ on
ⓒ at   ⓓ under

12 _____ beautiful garden!

ⓐ How   ⓑ What
ⓒ What a   ⓓ What an

[13-14] Look and choose.
그림을 보고, 알맞은 문장을 고르세요.

13

Jun. 13th

ⓐ The concert is on June 13th.

ⓑ The school market is on June 13th.

ⓒ The dance festival is on July 13th.

ⓓ The school market is on November 13th.

14

7F

ⓐ The bookstore is on the seventh floor.

ⓑ The computer room is on the second floor.

ⓒ The bookstore is on the sixth floor.

ⓓ The food court is on the seventh floor.

[15-16] Read and write the letter.
문장을 읽고, 알맞은 그림을 골라 기호를 쓰세요.

ⓐ   ⓑ
ⓒ   ⓓ

15 I want to join the music club. ☐

16 What an exciting game! ☐

[17-18] Fill in the blanks.
대화의 빈칸에 알맞은 말을 쓰세요.

17

A: _____ is the Christmas party?
B: It's _____ December 24th.

18

A: _____ is the art room?
B: It's _____ _____ fifth floor.

[19-20] Unscramble the sentence.
주어진 단어를 배열하여 문장을 쓰세요.

19

_____
(smart / a / robot / what / !)

20

A: _____
(grade / she / is / what / in / ?)
B: She's in the sixth grade.

Final TEST 5A

Institute

Name

Score   /100

[1-2] Listen and mark O or X.
다음을 듣고, ○ 또는 X를 표시하세요.

1

2

[3-5] Listen and write the letter.
다음을 듣고, 알맞은 그림의 기호를 쓰세요.

ⓐ   ⓑ   ⓒ   ⓓ

3 ☐   **4** ☐   **5** ☐

[6-7] Listen and choose.
다음을 듣고, 질문에 알맞은 응답을 고르세요.

6

ⓐ   ⓑ   ⓒ   ⓓ

7

ⓐ   ⓑ   ⓒ   ⓓ

[8-9] Listen and choose.
대화를 듣고, 알맞은 그림을 고르세요.

8   ⓐ    ⓑ

ⓒ    ⓓ

9   ⓐ    ⓑ

ⓒ    ⓓ

10 Listen and choose.
대화를 듣고, 질문에 알맞은 응답을 고르세요.

What did Jenny do last weekend?

ⓐ She ate spaghetti.

ⓑ She went to the farm.

ⓒ She saw paintings.

ⓓ She went to the museum.

[11-12] Read and choose.
빈칸에 알맞은 것을 고르세요.

11

> Can you come _____ the singing contest?

ⓐ in   ⓑ on
ⓒ at   ⓓ to

12

> I went to the festival.
> I _____ many pictures.

ⓐ took   ⓑ take
ⓒ takes   ⓓ taking

[13-15] Look and choose.
그림을 보고, 알맞은 문장을 골라 기호를 쓰세요.

> ⓐ She has brown eyes.
> ⓑ I'll go there by bike.
> ⓒ I went to the museum.
> ⓓ Can you come to my birthday party?
> ⓔ She has long curly hair.

13

14

15

16 Look and choose.
그림을 보고, 알맞은 문장을 고르세요.

ⓐ I went to the zoo.
ⓑ I picked tomatoes.
ⓒ I saw paintings.
ⓓ I went to the food festival.

[17-18] Unscramble the sentence.
주어진 단어를 배열하여 문장을 쓰세요.

17

> _____
> (hair / she / long / straight / has / .)

18

> _____
> (went / I / to / yesterday / the farm / .)

[19-20] Fill in the blanks.
대화의 빈칸에 알맞은 말을 쓰세요.

19

> A: Can you _____ _____ the fireworks festival?
> B: Of _____. _____ is it?
> A: It's this Wednesday.

20

> A: I'll go to the library on Saturday.
> B: How _____ _____ go there?
> A: I'll go there _____ foot.

2nd Edition

LET'S GO

to the English World

5A

Word Book
& Workbook

CHUNJAE EDUCATION, INC.

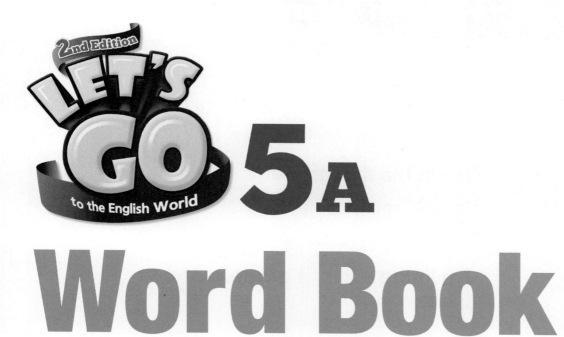

Word Book

5A

to the English World

2nd Edition

UNIT **1** ············· 2

UNIT **5** ············· 10

UNIT **2** ············· 4

UNIT **6** ············· 12

UNIT **3** ············· 6

UNIT **7** ············· 14

UNIT **4** ············· 8

UNIT **8** ············· 16

UNIT 1 I'm in the Sixth Grade

first 첫 번째(의)	**I'm in the first grade.** 나는 1학년이야.
second 두 번째(의)	**I'm in the second grade.** 나는 2학년이야.
third 세 번째(의)	**He's in the third grade.** 그는 3학년이야.
fourth 네 번째(의)	**She's in the fourth grade.** 그녀는 4학년이야.
fifth 다섯 번째(의)	**Are you in the fifth grade?** 너는 5학년이니?
sixth 여섯 번째(의)	**Is she in the sixth grade?** 그녀는 6학년이니?
grade 학년	**What grade are you in?** 너는 몇 학년이니?
spell 철자를 맞게 쓰다	**How do you spell your name?** 네 이름의 철자가 어떻게 되니?

B Read, write, and say.

1 first
첫 번째(의)

_____ _____ _____

2 second
두 번째(의)

_____ _____ _____

3 third
세 번째(의)

_____ _____ _____

4 fourth
네 번째(의)

_____ _____ _____

5 fifth
다섯 번째(의)

_____ _____ _____

6 sixth
여섯 번째(의)

_____ _____ _____

7 grade
학년

_____ _____ _____

8 spell
철자를 맞게 쓰다

_____ _____ _____

Learn More

same 같은	We're in the same grade. 우리는 같은 학년이야.
club 동아리	Let's join the club together. 함께 동아리에 가입하자.
join 가입하다	I want to join the dance club. 나는 댄스 동아리에 가입하고 싶어.
magic trick 마술 묘기	I like doing magic tricks. 나는 마술 묘기를 부리는 것을 좋아해.

Where Is the Science Room?

A Listen and repeat. 15 16

science room 과학실	**Where is the** science room**?** 과학실은 어디에 있니?
music room 음악실	**Where is the** music room**?** 음악실은 어디에 있니?
computer room 컴퓨터실	**Where is the** computer room**?** 컴퓨터실은 어디에 있니?
art room 미술실	**The** art room **is on the second floor.** 미술실은 2층에 있어.
flower shop 꽃집	**The** flower shop **is on the ninth floor.** 꽃집은 9층에 있어.
gift shop 선물 가게	**The** gift shop **is on the sixth floor.** 선물 가게는 6층에 있어.
movie theater 영화관	**It's next to the** movie theater**.** 그것은 영화관 옆에 있어.
food court 푸드 코트	**Let's go to the** food court **first.** 푸드 코트에 먼저 가자.

1 science room
과학실

2 computer room
컴퓨터실

3 art room
미술실

4 music room
음악실

5 flower shop
꽃집

6 gift shop
선물 가게

7 food court
푸드 코트

8 movie theater
영화관

Learn More

first 첫 번째(의)	**second** 두 번째(의)	**third** 세 번째(의)	**fourth** 네 번째(의)	**building** 건물	**restroom** 화장실
fifth 다섯 번째(의)	**sixth** 여섯 번째(의)	**seventh** 일곱 번째(의)	**eighth** 여덟 번째(의)	**elevator** 엘리베이터	**floor** 층
ninth 아홉 번째(의)	**tenth** 열 번째(의)			**bank** 은행	

What a Nice Picture!

A Listen and repeat. 🎧29 🎧30

nice house 멋진 집	**Look at the** nice house. 멋진 집을 봐.
cute baby 귀여운 아기	**Look at the** cute baby. 귀여운 아기를 봐.
tall tower 높은 탑	**It's a** tall tower. 그것은 높은 탑이야.
exciting game 흥미진진한 경기	**It's an** exciting game. 그것은 흥미진진한 경기야.
old book 오래된 책	**What an** old book! 정말 오래된 책이구나!
beautiful garden 아름다운 정원	**What a** beautiful garden! 정말 아름다운 정원이구나!
funny movie 웃긴 영화	**What a** funny movie! 정말 웃긴 영화구나!
big fish 큰 물고기	**What a** big fish! 정말 큰 물고기구나!

B Read, write, and say.

☐ Read ☐ Write ☐ Say

1 nice house
멋진 집

_____ _____ _____

2 cute baby
귀여운 아기

_____ _____ _____

3 tall tower
높은 탑

_____ _____ _____

4 exciting game
흥미진진한 경기

_____ _____ _____

5 old book
오래된 책

_____ _____ _____

6 beautiful garden
아름다운 정원

_____ _____ _____

7 funny movie
웃긴 영화

_____ _____ _____

8 big fish
큰 물고기

_____ _____ _____

Learn More

big brush
큰 붓

That's a big brush.
그거 큰 붓이구나.

nice picture
멋진 그림

What a nice picture!
정말 멋진 그림이구나!

smart robot
똑똑한 로봇

What a smart robot!
정말 똑똑한 로봇이구나!

When Is Dad's Birthday?

A **Listen and repeat.** 43 44

January 1월	**It's on** January **10th.** 그것은 1월 10일이야.
February 2월	**It's on** February **3rd.** 그것은 2월 3일이야.
March 3월	**It's on** March **22nd.** 그것은 3월 22일이야.
April 4월	**The school festival is on** April **15th.** 학교 축제는 4월 15일이야.
May 5월	**Jason's birthday is on** May **5th.** 제이슨의 생일은 5월 5일이야.
June 6월	**My birthday is on** June **23rd.** 내 생일은 6월 23일이야.
July 7월	**The movie festival is on** July **4th.** 영화 축제는 7월 4일이야.
August 8월	**The dance festival is on** August **30th.** 댄스 축제는 8월 30일이야.
September 9월	**Mom's birthday is on** September **9th.** 엄마의 생신은 9월 9일이야.
October 10월	**Halloween Day is on** October **31st.** 핼러윈 데이는 10월 31일이야.
November 11월	**The school market is on** November **12th.** 학교 장터는 11월 12일이야.
December 12월	**Christmas Day is on** December **25th.** 크리스마스는 12월 25일이야.

1 January
1월

2 February
2월

3 March
3월

4 April
4월

5 May
5월

6 June
6월

7 July
7월

8 August
8월

9 September
9월

10 October
10월

11 November
11월

12 December
12월

Learn More

when 언제	When is Dad's birthday? 아빠의 생신이 언제니?
birthday party 생일 파티	When is Kevin's birthday party? 케빈의 생일 파티가 언제니?
concert 콘서트	The concert is on May 4th. 콘서트는 5월 4일이야.

A **Listen and repeat.** 57 58

sports day 체육대회	**When is the** sports day**?** 체육대회가 언제니?
piano concert 피아노 콘서트	**When is the** piano concert**?** 피아노 콘서트가 언제니?
fireworks festival 불꽃놀이 축제	**The** fireworks festival **is tomorrow.** 불꽃놀이 축제는 내일이야.
singing contest 노래 경연대회	**The** singing contest **is on April 5th.** 노래 경연대회는 4월 5일이야.
magic show 마술 쇼	**The** magic show **is this Friday.** 마술 쇼는 이번 주 금요일이야.
art contest 미술 경연대회	**Can you come to the** art contest**?** 미술 경연대회에 올 수 있니?
Christmas party 크리스마스 파티	**Can you come to the** Christmas party**?** 크리스마스 파티에 올 수 있니?
basketball game 농구 경기	**Can you come to the** basketball game**?** 농구 경기에 올 수 있니?

B Read, write, and say.

1 sports day
체육대회

2 piano concert
피아노 콘서트

3 fireworks festival
불꽃놀이 축제

4 singing contest
노래 경연대회

5 magic show
마술 쇼

6 art contest
미술 경연대회

7 Christmas party
크리스마스 파티

8 basketball game
농구 경기

Learn More

enjoy
즐기다

We can enjoy many games.
우리는 많은 게임들을 즐길 수 있어.

Halloween party
핼러윈 파티

When is the Halloween party?
핼러윈 파티가 언제니?

meet
만나다

Let's meet at 6.
6시에 만나자.

What Did You Do Last Weekend?

Ⓐ **Listen and repeat.** 71 72

played in the sand 모래밭에서 놀았다	**I** played in the sand. 나는 모래밭에서 놀았어.
picked tomatoes 토마토를 땄다	**I** picked tomatoes **there.** 나는 거기에서 토마토를 땄어.
saw paintings 그림들을 보았다	**She** saw paintings **at the museum.** 그녀는 박물관에서 그림들을 보았어.
took many pictures 사진을 많이 찍었다	**We** took many pictures **in Paris.** 우리는 파리에서 사진을 많이 찍었어.
saw my favorite singer 내가 가장 좋아하는 가수를 보았다	**I** saw my favorite singer **on Saturday.** 나는 토요일에 내가 가장 좋아하는 가수를 보았어.
bought new clothes 새 옷을 샀다	**They** bought new clothes **yesterday.** 그들은 어제 새 옷을 샀어.

1 played in the sand
모래밭에서 놀았다

_____   _____

2 picked tomatoes
토마토를 땄다

_____   _____

3 saw paintings
그림들을 보았다

_____   _____

4 took many pictures
사진을 많이 찍었다

_____   _____

5 saw my favorite singer
내가 가장 좋아하는 가수를 보았다

_____   _____

6 bought new clothes
새 옷을 샀다

_____   _____

Learn More

during the vacation
방학 동안에

What did you do during the vacation?
너는 방학 동안에 무엇을 했니?

last weekend
지난 주말에

I went to a basketball game last weekend.
나는 지난 주말에 농구 경기를 보러 갔어.

met
만났다

Alex met his friends.
알렉스는 그의 친구들을 만났어.

went
갔다

Mina went to the fish festival.
미나는 물고기 축제에 갔어.

beach
해변

They went to the beach.
그들은 해변에 갔어.

She Has Short Curly Hair

Ⓐ **Listen and repeat.** 85 86

short hair 짧은 머리	**Mr. Smith has** short hair. 스미스 씨는 짧은 머리를 하고 있어.
long hair 긴 머리	**She has** long hair. 그녀는 긴 머리를 하고 있어.
straight hair 생머리	**I have** straight hair. 나는 생머리를 하고 있어.
curly hair 곱슬머리	**He has long** curly hair. 그는 긴 곱슬머리를 하고 있어.
blue eyes 파란색 눈	**Her cat has** blue eyes. 그녀의 고양이는 파란색 눈을 가지고 있어.
green eyes 초록색 눈	**My uncle has** green eyes. 나의 삼촌은 초록색 눈을 가지고 있어.
brown eyes 갈색 눈	**They have** brown eyes. 그들은 갈색 눈을 가지고 있어.

1 short hair
짧은 머리

_____ _____ _____

2 long hair
긴 머리

_____ _____ _____

3 straight hair
생머리

_____ _____ _____

4 curly hair
곱슬머리

_____ _____ _____

5 blue eyes
파란색 눈

_____ _____ _____

6 green eyes
초록색 눈

_____ _____ _____

7 brown eyes
갈색 눈

_____ _____ _____

Learn More

find 찾다	I can't find my sister. 나는 내 여동생을 찾을 수가 없어.
wear 입다	What is he wearing? 그는 무엇을 입고 있니?
look like ~처럼 보이다	What does she look like? 그녀는 어떻게 생겼니?

How Will You Go There?

(A) **Listen and repeat.** 99 100

by bus 버스를 타고	**I go to school** by bus. 나는 학교에 버스를 타고 가.
by subway 지하철을 타고	**We went to the zoo** by subway. 우리는 동물원에 지하철을 타고 갔어.
by car 자동차를 타고	**They went there** by car. 그들은 거기에 자동차를 타고 갔어.
by train 기차를 타고	**He went to the farm** by train. 그는 농장에 기차를 타고 갔어.
by bike 자전거를 타고	**I'll go to the park** by bike. 나는 공원에 자전거를 타고 갈 거야.
on foot 걸어서	**She'll go to school** on foot. 그녀는 학교에 걸어서 갈 거야.
by ship 배를 타고	**Dad will go to China** by ship. 아빠는 중국에 배를 타고 갈 거야.
by plane 비행기를 타고	**Fred will go there** by plane. 프레드는 거기에 비행기를 타고 갈 거야.

1 by bus
버스를 타고

2 by subway
지하철을 타고

3 by car
자동차를 타고

4 by train
기차를 타고

5 by bike
자전거를 타고

6 on foot
걸어서

7 by ship
배를 타고

8 by plane
비행기를 타고

Learn More

market 시장	She goes to the market by bike. 그녀는 시장에 자전거를 타고 가.
airport 공항	He'll go to the airport by subway. 그는 공항에 지하철을 타고 갈 거야.
mountain 산	I'll go to the mountain by bus. 나는 산에 버스를 타고 갈 거야.

Workbook

UNIT **1** · · · · · · · · · · · · · 20

UNIT **2** · · · · · · · · · · · · · 26

UNIT **3** · · · · · · · · · · · · · 32

UNIT **4** · · · · · · · · · · · · · 38

UNIT **5** · · · · · · · · · · · · · 44

UNIT **6** · · · · · · · · · · · · · 50

UNIT **7** · · · · · · · · · · · · · 56

UNIT **8** · · · · · · · · · · · · · 62

I'm in the Sixth Grade

Words

A Unscramble the word.

① 1st ② 2nd ③ 3rd ④ 4th ⑤ 5th ⑥ 6th

1 t f s r i _____

2 o s n c d e _____

3 i t d h r _____

4 u f r h t o _____

5 h f i t f _____

6 x s t i h _____

B Circle and write.

1

I'm in the _____ grade.
(fourth/ third)

2

I'm in the _____ grade.
(first / third)

3

I'm in the _____ grade.
(fifth/ sixth)

Practice

(A) Look and write.

1

I'm Grace.

I'm in the _____ grade.

2

My name is Jade.

I'm in the _____.

3

I'm Jake.

I'm _____.

(B) Read and choose.

1

What grade are you in?

ⓐ I'm in the first grade.

ⓑ I'm in the third grade.

2

What grade are you in?

ⓐ I'm in the sixth grade.

ⓑ I'm in the fifth grade.

3

What grade are you in?

ⓐ I'm in the sixth grade.

ⓑ I'm in the second grade.

4

What grade are you in?

ⓐ I'm in the third grade.

ⓑ I'm in the first grade.

Write & Talk

Ⓐ Read and match.

1 What grade are you in? •

ⓐ • T-H-O-M-A-S.

2 Are you in the second grade? •

ⓑ • I'm in the sixth grade.

3 How do you spell your name? •

ⓒ • No, I'm not.
I'm in the first grade.

Ⓑ Read and write.

1

A: What grade is he in?

B: He's in _____.

2

A: What grade is she in?

B: She's in _____.

3

A: I'm in _____.

B: Really? We're in the same grade.

4

I'm in _____.

I want to join the dance club.

Reading

A Read and write T or F.

1 Her name is Joy. ☐

2 She's in the fourth grade. ☐

3 She likes doing magic tricks. ☐

4 She wants to join the movie club. ☐

B Read and write.

1

Name Kate   Grade 4th

School Club cooking club

Hi, I'm Kate.

I'm in the _____ grade.

I want to join the _____ club.

2

Name Tom   Grade 3rd

School Club sports club

Hi, my name is Tom.

I'm in _____.

I want to join _____.

3

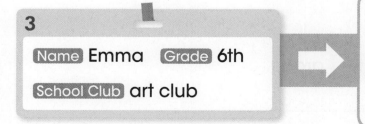

Name Emma   Grade 6th

School Club art club

Hello, I'm Emma.

I'm _____.

I want to _____.

Build Up

A Look and write.

1 one — first

2 two — [____]

3 three — [____]

4 four — [____]

5 five — [____]

6 six — [____]

B Change and rewrite.

1

I'm in the `two` grade.

···▸ _____

2

She's in the `four` grade.

···▸ _____

3

He's in the `one` grade.

···▸ _____

4

They're in the `five` grade.

···▸ _____

Writing

Ⓐ Make the sentence.

1 _____

(sixth grade / in / I'm / the / .) 나는 6학년이야.

2 _____

(in / third grade / the / my brother / is / .) 나의 남동생은 3학년이야.

3 _____

(you / are / in / what grade / ?) 너는 몇 학년이니?

4 _____

(in / the / you / second grade / are / ?) 너는 2학년이니?

5 _____

(same grade / in / the / we're / .) 우리는 같은 학년이야.

6 _____

(to join / I / the dance club / want / .) 나는 댄스 동아리에 가입하고 싶어.

7 _____

(spell / your name / do you / how / ?) 네 이름의 철자는 어떻게 되니?

Words

(A) Look and circle.

1

music room | art room

2

computer room | science room

3

flower shop | gift shop

4

food court | movie theater

(B) Look and write.

| gift shop | movie theater | computer room |

1

Where is the _____?

2

Where is the _____?

3

Excuse me. Where is the _____?

Practice

(A) Read and match.

1 Where is the food court?  ⓐ It's on the third floor.

2 Where is the music room?  ⓑ It's on the tenth floor.

3 Where is the gift shop?  ⓒ It's on the sixth floor.

(B) Look and circle.

1

A: Where is the (computer room / art room)?

B: It's on the (seventh / second) floor.

2

A: Where is the (flower shop / movie theater)?

B: It's on the (ninth / fifth) floor.

3

A: Where is the (art room / science room)?

B: It's on the (fourth / first) floor.

Write & Talk

A Write and choose.

1

Where is the _____?

ⓐ It's on the tenth floor.

ⓑ It's on the eighth floor.

2

Where is the _____?

ⓐ It's on the first floor.

ⓑ It's on the second floor.

3

Where is the _____?

ⓐ It's on the third floor.

ⓑ It's on the fourth floor.

4

Where is the _____?

ⓐ Go to the seventh floor, please.

ⓑ Go to the ninth floor, please.

B Read and write the letter.

1

A: Excuse me. _____( )_____

B: It's on the eighth floor.

_____( )_____

A: Thank you.

2

A: Jack, what grade are you in?

B: _____( )_____

A: Where is your classroom?

B: _____( )_____

ⓐ It's next to the gift shop.　ⓑ It's on the fourth floor.

ⓒ I'm in the sixth grade.　ⓓ Where is the food court?

28

Reading

Ⓐ Read and write.

the first floor
two elevators
game room
a movie theater

This is the new building.

1 There are _____.

2 There's a bank on _____.

3 The _____ is on the ninth floor.

4 There's _____ on the tenth floor.

Ⓑ Look and write.

1

There's a _____ on the _____.

2

The _____ is on the _____.

3

There's a _____ on _____.

4

The _____ is _____ the _____.

Build Up

A Look and write.

Happy Building

7F Toy Shop
5F Food Court
3F Bookstore
1F Supermarket

1 There's a food court _____ the _____ floor.

2 There's a bookstore _____ the _____ floor.

3 There's a supermarket _____ the _____ floor.

4 There's a toy shop _____ the _____ floor.

B Change and rewrite.

1

9F

The science room is on the `nineth` floor.

···▶ _____

2

4F

My classroom is on the `four` floor.

···▶ _____

3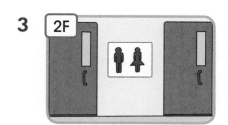

2F

The restrooms are on the `twoth` floor.

···▶ _____

4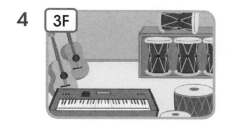

3F

The music room is on the `threeth` floor.

···▶ _____

Writing

A Make the sentence.

1 _____

(the art room / is / where / ?) 미술실이 어디에 있니?

2 _____

(is / where / the gift shop / ?) 선물 가게가 어디에 있나요?

3 _____

(the eighth floor / on / it's / .) 그것은 8층에 있어.

4 _____

(it's / the bookstore / next to / .) 그것은 서점 옆에 있어.

5 _____

(on / the food court / the second floor / is / .) 푸드 코트는 2층에 있어.

6 _____

(the tenth floor / is / on / the movie theater / .) 영화관은 10층에 있어.

7 _____

(the first floor / there's / on / a bank / .) 1층에 은행이 있어.

What a Nice Picture!

Words

A **Look and write the letter.**

ⓐ a nice house	ⓑ a cute baby	ⓒ a tall tower
ⓓ an old book	ⓔ a big fish	ⓕ an exciting game

1

2

3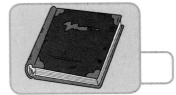

4

5

6

B **Look and circle.**

1

What a (funny movie / big fish)!

2

What a (tall tower / nice house)!

3

What a (cute baby / beautiful garden)!

Practice

Ⓐ Read and match.

1   What an exciting game!   •

   ⓐ

2   What a funny movie!   •

   ⓑ

3   What a nice picture!   •

   ⓒ

Ⓑ Look and write.

| a tall tower | an old book | a nice house | a cute baby |

1

What _____!

2

What _____!

3

What _____!

4

What _____!

Write & Talk

A Read and write the letter.

1

A: This is my school library.

B: _____ (   ) _____

There are many books.

2

A: Look at that fish.

It's very small.

B: _____ (   ) _____

3

A: Look at the garden.

There are beautiful flowers.

B: _____ (   ) _____

ⓐ What a beautiful garden!

ⓑ What a big library!

ⓒ What a small fish!

B Read and write.

1

A: What a _____ !

B: Yes. It's very funny.

2

A: There's a house. It's very old.

B: What an _____ !

3

A: Look at that building. It's very tall.

B: _____

Reading

Ⓐ Read and write.

Robby is my robot.

He is _____.

He can _____.

He can do _____, too.

What a _____!

| very nice | clean the house | smart robot | my homework |

Ⓑ Read and write.

1

This is my robot dog, Popo.

He can _____.

What a _____!

| many flowers |
| nice robot dog |

2

Look at the garden.

There are _____.

What a _____!

| play with a ball |
| beautiful garden |

Build Up

Ⓐ Read and match.

1 The tree is very tall.

ⓐ

ⓓ What a beautiful flower!

2 The cat is very cute.

ⓑ

ⓔ What a cute cat!

3 The flower is very beautiful.

ⓒ

ⓕ What a tall tree!

Ⓑ Read and write.

1

The bear is very big.

···▸ What _____!

2

The house is very old.

···▸ _____

3

The bird is very small.

···▸ _____

4

The movie is very exciting.

···▸ _____

A Make the sentence.

1 _____

(a / picture / what / nice / !) 정말 멋진 그림이구나!

2 _____

(game / an / what / exciting / !) 정말 흥미진진한 경기구나!

3 _____

(cute / what / baby / a / !) 정말 귀여운 아기구나!

4 _____

(a / beautiful / what / flower / !) 정말 아름다운 꽃이구나!

5 _____

(funny / what / a / movie / !) 정말 웃긴 영화구나!

6 _____

(robot / smart / a / what / !) 정말 똑똑한 로봇이구나!

7 _____

(a / what / book / big / !) 정말 큰 책이구나!

When Is Dad's Birthday?

Words

A Look and write.

June	November	February	October	March	December
August	September	April	May	July	January

Practice

A Look and write.

1

My birthday is on _____ 12th.

2

Dad's birthday is on _____ 2nd.

3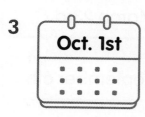

Anna's birthday is on _____ 1st.

B Read and write T or F.

1

When is your birthday?

It's on January 3rd. ☐

2

When is your birthday?

It's on June 21st. ☐

3

When is Dad's birthday?

It's on April 25th. ☐

4

When is Mom's birthday?

It's on October 10th. ☐

Write & Talk

A Read and match.

 Sep. 6th
 Mar. 23rd
 Dec. 25th
 Jan. 31st

1 When is the concert? •

ⓐ • It's on December 25th.

2 When is the school market? •

ⓑ • It's on March 23rd.

3 When is Christmas Day? •

ⓒ • It's on September 6th.

4 When is Mom's birthday? •

ⓓ • It's on January 31st.

B Read and write.

1 When is the school festival?

It's _____.

2 When is Halloween Day?

It's _____.

Oh, it's next Wednesday.

3 When is the movie festival?

It's _____.

Oh, that's today.

Jun. 12th
Oct. 31st
Aug. 14th

40

Reading

A **Read and number in the order.**

[2] I want to be a monster.
I'll wear a green mask.

[ ] Now, we're ready.
"Trick or treat!"

[ ] Today is October 31st.
It's Halloween Day!
We wear special clothes today.

[ ] Cindy wants to be a butterfly.
"I'll wear a yellow dress."

B **Read and match.**

1
Today is December 24th.
It's Christmas Eve.
I want a nice drone.

ⓐ
Dec. 24th

2
Mom's birthday is on February 22nd.
That's tomorrow.
I'll make a cake for Mom.

ⓑ
Aug. 15th

3
The dance festival is on August 15th.
That's today.
We can dance to the music.

ⓒ
Feb. 22nd

Build Up

A Read and choose.

1
eleven th
ⓐ 7th ⓑ 11th ⓒ 21st

2
thirteenth
ⓐ 13th ⓑ 25th ⓒ 30th

3
twentieth
ⓐ 12th ⓑ 20th ⓒ 22nd

4
thirty first
ⓐ 11th ⓑ 21st ⓒ 31st

5
twelfth
ⓐ 6th ⓑ 10th ⓒ 12th

6
twenty second
ⓐ 12th ⓑ 22nd ⓒ 27th

B Look and write.

1 My birthday is on _____.

2 The school market is on _____.

3 Halloween Day is on _____.

4 The piano concert is on _____.

5 The dance festival is on _____.

Mar. 1st

Jun. 22nd

Oct. 31st

Nov. 15th

Aug. 23rd

Writing

Ⓐ Make the sentence.

1 _____

(your / is / birthday / when / ?) 너의 생일은 언제니?

2 _____

(the school festival / when / is / ?) 학교 축제는 언제니?

3 _____

(22nd / it's / December / on / .) 그것은 12월 22일이야.

4 _____

(on / my birthday / is / 23rd / February / .) 내 생일은 2월 23일이야.

5 _____

(May / is / 12th / the piano concert / on / .) 피아노 콘서트는 5월 12일이야.

6 _____

(April / is / the school market / 10th / on / .) 학교 장터는 4월 10일이야.

7 _____

(is / Friday / next / Christmas Day / .) 크리스마스는 다음 주 금요일이야.

Can You Come to the Sports Day?

Words

A Look and write.

| piano concert | fireworks festival | magic show |
| sports day | art contest | Christmas party |

1

_____

2

_____

3

_____

4

_____

5

_____

6

_____

B Look and check.

1

☐ dance contest
☐ singing contest

2

☐ soccer game
☐ basketball game

3

☐ fireworks festival
☐ magic show

Practice

A Circle and write.

1

Can you come to the _____?

(sports day / singing contest)

2

Can you come to the _____?

(art contest / basketball game)

3

Can you come to the _____?

(fireworks festival / magic show)

B Write and check.

1

A: Can you come to the _____?

B: ☐ Of course. ☐ Sorry, I can't.

2

A: Can you come to the _____?

B: ☐ Of course. ☐ Sorry, I can't.

3

A: Can you come to the _____?

B: ☐ Of course. ☐ Sorry, I can't.

Write & Talk

A Read and write.

1
next Tuesday

A: Can you come to the _____?

B: Sure. When is it?

A: It's _____.

2
Dec. 24th

A: Can you come to the Christmas party?

It's on _____.

B: _____ See you then.

3
Concert
this Sunday

A: When is the _____?

B: It's this Sunday. Can you come to the concert?

A: _____ I'm busy.

| next Tuesday | piano concert | singing contest |
| December 24th | Sorry, I can't. | Of course. |

B Read and number in the order.

2 | Oh, it's this Saturday.

☐ | Can you come to the festival?

☐ | The fireworks festival is on May 8th.

☐ | Okay. See you then.

☐ | Sure. I like fireworks. Let's meet at 6 o'clock.

Reading

(A) Read and write.

eating contest
When: September 2nd, 3 P.M.
Where: Smile Park

Can you come to the _____ ?

The contest is on _____ .

You can eat many hot dogs.

Please come to _____ at 3.

Don't be late.

(B) Read and write T or F.

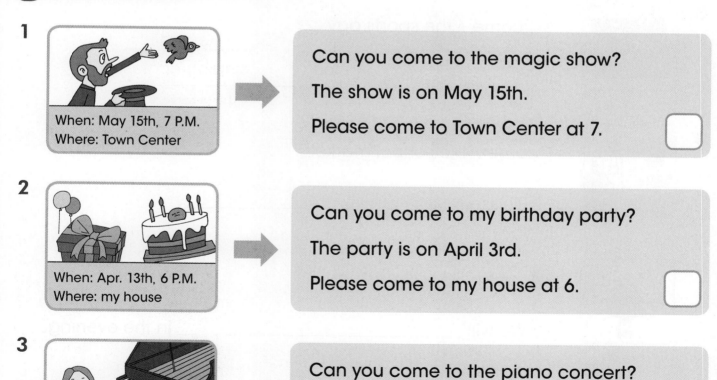

1

When: May 15th, 7 P.M.
Where: Town Center

Can you come to the magic show?

The show is on May 15th.

Please come to Town Center at 7.

2

When: Apr. 13th, 6 P.M.
Where: my house

Can you come to my birthday party?

The party is on April 3rd.

Please come to my house at 6.

3

When: Nov. 24th, 8 P.M.
Where: Concert Hall

Can you come to the piano concert?

It's November 24th.

Please come to Concert Hall at 8.

Build Up

A Complete the sentence.

come / my birthday party

····▸ Can you <u>come to my birthday party</u>?

1

come / the piano contest

····▸ Can you _____?

2

come / the singing contest

····▸ Can you _____?

3

come / the sports day

····▸ Dad, please _____.

4

come / the school market

····▸ Please _____.

5

go / the Christmas party

····▸ We will _____ in the evening.

6

go / the art contest

····▸ Cindy will _____.

A Make the sentence.

1 _____

(my birthday party / come / you / can / to / ?) 너는 내 생일 파티에 올 수 있니?

2 _____

(you / come / the singing contest / to / can / ?) 너는 노래 경연대회에 올 수 있니?

3 _____

(on / is / the magic show / August 10th / .) 마술 쇼는 8월 10일이야.

4 _____

(is / May 8th / the festival / on / .) 그 축제는 5월 8일이야.

5 _____

(is / the party / May 15th / on / .) 그 파티는 5월 15일이야.

6 _____

(please / at 3 / my house / to / come / .) 3시에 우리집에 오세요.

7 _____

(come / please / to / the school festival / .) 학교 축제에 오세요.

What Did You Do Last Weekend?

Words

Ⓐ Look and match.

1

ⓐ farm

ⓓ saw paintings

2

ⓑ museum

ⓔ saw my favorite singer

3

ⓒ concert

ⓕ picked tomatoes

Ⓑ Choose and write.

1

_____ in the sand

2

_____ new clothes

played

bought

took

3

_____ many pictures

4

_____ soccer

Practice

A Look and circle.

1  I (took / played) soccer with my friends.

2  I went to the (concert / shopping mall).
I (bought / met) new clothes.

3  I went to the (farm / museum).
I (picked / took) tomatoes.

B Read and write the letter.

ⓐ    ⓑ    ⓒ    ⓓ

1
A: What did you do last weekend?
B: I went to the museum.
I saw paintings. ☐

2
A: What did you do last weekend?
B: I went to the concert.
I saw my favorite singer. ☐

3
A: What did you do last weekend?
B: I went to the festival.
I took many pictures. ☐

4
A: What did you do last weekend?
B: I went to the beach.
I played in the sand. ☐

Write & Talk

A Circle, choose, and write.

saw	picked	new clothes	apples
took	bought	many animals	many pictures

1

A: What did you do last weekend?.

B: I went to the (shopping mall / farm).

I _____.

2

A: What did you do last Saturday?

B: I went to the (beach / zoo).

I _____.

3

A: What did you do yesterday?

B: I went to the (museum / festival).

I _____.

4

A: What did you do during the vacation?

B: I visited my uncle's (concert / farm).

I _____.

B Read and match.

1   How was your vacation?   •

ⓐ •   I went to the food festival.

2   What did you do?   •

ⓑ •   Yes, I did. I ate spaghetti.

3   Did you eat delicious food?   •

ⓒ •   It was great.

52

Reading

A Read, and write.

A: I came to Paris last Sunday.

B: _____

A: I went to the museum.

_____

B: _____

A: Yes, I did. I took many pictures.

I saw famous paintings.

Did you go to the Eiffel Tower?

What did you do there?

B Read and choose.

last weekend

last summer

during the vacation

1   What did you do during the vacation?

ⓐ I went to the museum.   ⓑ I went to the concert.

2   What did you do last summer?

ⓐ I swam at the beach.   ⓑ I visited the museum.

3   What did you do last weekend?

ⓐ I went to the shopping mall.   ⓑ I went to the farm.

Build Up

Ⓐ Change and write.

1 | play | played |

2 | go | |

3 | buy | |

4 | listen | |

5 | visit | |

6 | meet | |

7 | pick | |

8 | eat | |

9 | see | |

10 | take | |

Ⓑ Change and rewrite.

1

She meets her friends yesterday.

···▸ _____

2

He goed to the farm last Saturday.

···▸ _____

3

I visit my grandparents last weekend.

···▸ _____

4

We taked many pictures at the festival.

···▸ _____

 Writing

Ⓐ Make the sentence.

1 _____

(you / last weekend / did / what / do / ?) 너는 지난 주말에 무엇을 했니?

2 _____

(do / during / what / the vacation / you / did / ?) 너는 방학 동안에 무엇을 했니?

3 _____

(delicious / eat / did / food / you / ?) 너는 맛있는 음식을 먹었니?

4 _____

(went / I / the beach / to / .) 나는 해변에 갔어.

5 _____

(clothes / bought / I / new / .) 나는 새 옷을 샀어.

6 _____

(I / yesterday / the museum / visited / .) 나는 어제 박물관을 방문했어.

7 _____

(a hamburger / ate / at the food court / I / .) 나는 푸드 코트에서 햄버거를 먹었어.

She Has Short Curly Hair

Words

A Look and match.

1

2

3

4

| short curly hair | short straight hair | long curly hair | long straight hair |

B Look and choose.

1

ⓐ long straight hair

ⓑ long curly hair

2

ⓐ short curly hair

ⓑ long curly hair

3

ⓐ short straight hair

ⓑ short curly hair

4

ⓐ long straight hair

ⓑ short straight hair

Practice

A Read and write.

① 파란색 ② 파란색 ③ 초록색 ④ 갈색

| long straight | short curly | blue eyes | green eyes |

1 She has _____ and short straight hair.

2 She has blue eyes and _____ hair.

3 She has _____ and long curly hair.

4 She has brown eyes and _____ hair.

B Read and write T or F.

1
파란색

What does he look like?
He has brown eyes.

2

What does she look like?
She has long straight hair.

3
파란색

What does she look like?
She has blue eyes and long curly hair.

Write & Talk

Ⓐ Read and match.

1
A: What does Chris look like?
B: He has straight hair.

ⓐ 갈색

2
A: What does Anna look like?
B: She has long straight hair.

ⓑ

3
A: What does James look like?
B: He has brown eyes and short curly hair.

ⓒ 파란색

4
A: What does Betty look like?
B: She has blue eyes and long curly hair.

ⓓ

Ⓑ Read and circle.

1

파란색

He has short black hair.

He's wearing a (blue T-shirt / red T-shirt).

2

She has (long straight hair / long curly hair).

She's wearing a red T-shirt.

3

초록색

He has gray and black hair.

He has big (green eyes / yellow eyes).

58

Reading

A Read and write.

1

He has _____ hair.

He has two sharp teeth.

He is wearing _____.

2

노란색

She has long hair.

She has _____.

She's wearing _____.

| big eyes | black clothes | a yellow dress | short black |

B Read and write the letter.

ⓐ  파란색

ⓑ  갈색

ⓒ  갈색

1

A: I can't find Amy.

B: What does she look like?

A: She has brown eyes and
long straight hair.

2

A: I can't find my sister.

B: What does she look like?

A: She has blue eyes and
short curly hair.

Build Up

Ⓐ Look and choose.

1  검은색

      ⓐ black short hair   ⓑ short black hair

2

      ⓐ long straight hair   ⓑ straight long hair

3  파란색

      ⓐ big blue eyes   ⓑ blue big eyes

4

      ⓐ curly short hair   ⓑ short curly hair

Ⓑ Unscramble the sentence.

1  갈색

My brother has _____.
       (brown / short / hair)

2

They have _____.
       (hair / long / straight)

3  노란색

The cat has _____.
       (yellow / big / eyes)

4 검은색

The dog has _____.
       (long / hair / black)

A Make the sentence.

1 _____

(he / what / like / does / look / ?) 그는 어떻게 생겼니?

2 _____

(she / what / like / does / look / ?) 그녀는 어떻게 생겼니?

3 _____

(short / he / hair / has / straight / .) 그는 짧은 생머리를 하고 있어.

4 _____

(hair / long / she / curly / has / .) 그녀는 긴 곱슬머리를 하고 있어.

5 _____

(she / blue eyes / long / has / brown hair / and / .) 그녀는 파란색 눈과 긴 갈색 머리를 하고 있어.

6 _____

(has / curly hair / and / brown eyes / he / short / .) 그는 갈색 눈과 짧은 곱슬머리를 하고 있어.

7 _____

(wearing / yellow boots / she's / .) 그녀는 노란색 부츠를 신고 있어.

How Will You Go There?

Words

Ⓐ Look and write the letter.

| ⓐ by train | ⓑ by bus | ⓒ by plane | ⓓ by bike |
| ⓔ by ship | ⓕ by car | ⓖ by subway | ⓗ on foot |

1 　　2 　　3 　　4

5 　　6 　　7 　　8

Ⓑ Look and circle.

1

I'll go to the (zoo / library).

I'll go there by (subway / car).

2

I'll go to (China / Canada).

I'll go there by (plane / ship).

3

I'll go to the (market / museum).

I'll go there by (car / bike).

Practice

Ⓐ Match and write.

by car   by train   on foot

1   I'll go to the farm. •

Ⓐ  •   I'll go there _____.

2   I'll go to the museum. •

Ⓑ  •   I'll go there _____.

3   I'll go to the beach. •

ⓒ •   I'll go there _____.

Ⓑ Read and write.

1

A: I'll go to Japan.

B: How will you go there?

A: I'll go there _____.

2

A: I'll go to the _____.

B: How will you go there?

A: I'll go there _____.

3

A: I'll go to the _____.

B: How will you go there?

A: I'll go there _____.

4

A: I'll go to New York.

B: How will you go there?

A: I'll go there _____.

Write & Talk

A Match and write.

1

ⓐ
A: I'll go to the market.

B: How _____ you go there?

A: I'll go there _____.

2

ⓑ
A: I'll go to the shopping mall.

B: How _____ go there?

A: I'll go there _____.

3

ⓒ
A: I'll go to Paris.

B: _____ will you _____ there?

A: I'll go there _____.

B Read and number in the order.

| 1 | What will you do tomorrow? |

☐ I'll go there by bus.
Can you join me?

☐ I'll go to the toy shop.

☐ Sorry, I can't. I'm busy tomorrow.

☐ How will you go there?

Reading

A Read and write the letter.

_____ (   )

How will I go there?

_____ (   )

I'm in the bike riding club.

_____ (   )

It was fun and exciting.

We love to travel by bike.

ⓐ I'll go to Canada this summer.

ⓑ We went to L.A. by bike last year.

ⓒ I'll go there by bike.

B Read and write T or F.

1.
I'll go to Australia this summer.
I'll go there by ship.

2.
I'll go to Paris this vacation.
I'll travel on foot.

3.
I went to my uncle's farm last weekend.
I went there by train.

4.
John will go to Japan next Monday.
He will go there by plane.

Build Up

Ⓐ Read and match.

1 by car   **2** by ship   **3** by train   **4** by bus

 ⓐ
 ⓑ
 ⓒ
 ⓓ

Ⓑ Look and write.

1

Mom goes to the market _____.

2

I'll go to Grand Park _____.

3

She went to the U.S. _____.

4

We went to the tower _____.

A Make the sentence.

1 _____

(you / how / will / there / go / ?) 너는 거기에 어떻게 갈거니?

2 _____

(go / I'll / by subway / there / .) 나는 거기에 지하철을 타고 갈 거야.

3 _____

(go / the beach / I'll / tomorrow / to / .) 나는 내일 해변에 갈 거야.

4 _____

(the market / go / to / on foot / I'll / .) 나는 시장에 걸어서 갈 거야.

5 _____

(to / I'll / the farm / by bus / go / .) 나는 농장에 버스를 타고 갈 거야.

6 _____

(by bike / went / L.A. / last year / we / to / .) 우리는 작년에 L.A.에 자전거를 타고 갔어.

7 _____

(we / to travel / by bike / love / .) 우리는 자전거를 타고 여행하는 것을 좋아해.